One Minute, Mama

A CHILL GUIDE FOR MOMS

ZADIE DAWSON

The boring stuff...

Copyright © 2025
All rights reserved.
No portion of this book may be reproduced
in any form without written permission
from the publisher or author, except as
permitted by U.S. copyright law.

INTRODUCTION

Why I Wrote This ?

(In a Blur Between School Runs and Cold Coffee)

I didn't write this book because I'm some zen guru who floats through life on a cloud of lavender essential oil.

I wrote it because one day, I found myself standing in the kitchen, reheating the same cup of coffee for the third time, while one child screamed about a sock and the other was asking life's big question like:

"why do we have eyebrows?"

I hadn't sat down all day.

I hadn't taken a full breath, looked out the window, or done one single thing that felt like me.

I hadn't even peed in peace

and let's be honest, that's a luxury now.

That night (after the bedtime battle, snack negotiations, and existential dishwasher loading),

I Googled

> 🔍 mindfulness for moms.　　　　　　　✕

Everything I found assumed I had 20 minutes of silence and a scenic view. What I actually had?

Sixty seconds and a bathroom that doubles as a panic room.

This book is a collection of those one-minute moments. They're quick. They're simple.

And they're made for you - the mama with no time, a full heart, and possibly some mashed banana on her shirt.

You don't need more pressure, another routine to fail at, or a checklist that makes you feel behind. You just need a few tiny, doable ways to feel more human in the middle of it all.

Let's be mindful - not perfect.

You in?

Zadie x

1

WHAT MINDFULNESS ISN'T

Spoiler: It's Not About Perfectly Arranged Crystals

Let's just clear this up straight away: mindfulness isn't reserved for monks, yoga instructors, or that one mom in your group who swears by sage smudging and never raises her voice (how??).

What Mindfulness Isn't:

- ✗ Sitting cross-legged on a mountain

- ✗ Chanting "Om" while the sun rises

- ✗ Having an immaculate, Pinterest-worthy meditation corner

- ✗ Or even sitting still for more than 90 seconds

If you've ever rolled your eyes at a guided meditation that starts with "find a quiet place where you won't be disturbed," you're not alone.

Where?

In my dreams?

The bathroom with the door locked and a child shouting under it?

Mindfulness has been dressed up in a lot of packaging that just doesn't fit real mom life.

BUT HERE'S THE THING: IT'S NOT ABOUT CANDLES OR SILENCE OR DOING IT "RIGHT."

It's about not totally losing your mind when you step on Lego barefoot while holding a toddler and boiling pasta.

IT'S ABOUT PRESENCE.

Pausing, even briefly, to notice what's happening. No judgment. No fixing. Just noticing. That's it.

And if you happen to be holding a glass of wine or hiding in the pantry while you do it — still counts.

2

WHY ONE MINUTE WORKS

(Because That's Literally All You've Got)

Look, if I had time for a 10-minute morning routine involving meditation, journaling, affirmations, and a gratitude walk... I'd be a whole new woman. But I don't. And chances are, neither do you.

✧ We're moms. ✧

Time gets swallowed by snacks, school bags, and that eternal search for the missing shoe.

So let's stop pretending we have "extra" time and start using the scraps we do have.

# Here's the good news:

Studies show that even short moments of mindfulness as little as 60 seconds, It can:

✓ Reduce stress

✓ Improve focus

✓ Lower your heart rate

✓ Increase patience (handy when your kid asks you "why" 57 times)

Micro-mindfulness isn't a cop-out. It's strategic.

A minute is short enough to squeeze in, but long enough to shift your state.

Think of it like a mental reset button. You don't need to overhaul your life. You just need to sprinkle in a few of these one-minute pauses throughout your day. The impact stacks up.

Like a savings account for your sanity.

Also... let's not forget, you probably spend more than a minute scrolling Instagram or wondering if that cough is something or something... so yeah, one minute? We've got this.

3

YOUR LIFE IS THE PRACTICE

(Spoiler: You're Already Doing It)

The beauty of this whole approach is that you don't need to add anything. You just need to notice more of what you're already doing.

Because let's face it — moms are multitasking warriors. But all that doing means we rarely feel present. And that's where mindfulness sneaks in.

Brushing your teeth = Meditation.

You're already doing it. So slow it down. Feel the brush. Notice the taste. Breathe through your nose. Boom — you're meditating.

Folding laundry = Breathing practice.

Don't rush. Don't think about the million other things. Just fold. Inhale. Exhale. Appreciate the quiet. (And if it's not quiet, appreciate that you're still folding.)

Screaming into a pillow = still counts.

Mindfulness doesn't mean you're calm all the time. It means you notice the chaos, let yourself feel it, and choose not to let it wreck you. Even if that means taking a moment to shout into a cushion like you're starring in a soap opera.

The point is: your life isn't getting in the way of mindfulness

-it is the practice. You don't need a retreat. You need a reminder.

SO HERE'S ONE: YOU'RE DOING GREAT.

EVEN WHEN YOU FEEL LIKE A MESS. ESPECIALLY THEN.

PART 2

The Minute Mama Moves

One-minute rituals for when peace feels impossible.

4

SIP AND CENTER

(Your coffee break just became a spiritual practice.)

You've finally made a coffee. Maybe even a warm one. Before you gulp it like it's medicine, try this:

Minute Mindfulness Practice:

- **Hold your mug with both hands.**
- **Feel the warmth, smell the steam.**
- **Take one slow sip.**
- **As you swallow, exhale through your nose.**
- **Whisper in your head: This is my moment.**

That's it. The world can wait 60 seconds. Even if the microwave is beeping and a small person is asking for a snack.

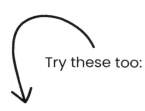
Try these too:

- **Take 3 mindful sips before picking up your phone.**
- **Stir your drink slowly and notice the swirl.**
- **Close your eyes for just one breath while holding your mug.**

Reheating leftovers?

While you wait for that "ding," place a hand on your belly and just breathe.

Microwave = mindfulness timer.

5

THE "DON'T LOSE IT" BREATH

(A one-minute meltdown diffuser.)

You're on the brink. Everyone's whining. Someone spilled something. You can feel it rising.
Stop. Breathe.

Minute Mindfulness Practice: Box Breathing

- **Inhale for 4 counts**
- **Hold for 4 counts**
- **Exhale for 4 counts**
- **Hold for 4 counts**
- **Repeat 3 times = 48 seconds of pure regulation.**

Or try:

- **Blowing slow, steady "dragon breaths" like your child's birthday candles are still lit**
- **Sighing out loud – the dramatic, over-the-top kind**
- **Saying "inhale…exhale…" out loud as you do it (yes, even with a kid watching)**

Your breath is always with you. And it's free. Use it like a superpower. Especially when you're ready to scream.

6

BE WHERE YOUR FEET ARE
(Grounding in the chaos, crumbs and all.)

You're in the kitchen. Or the car. Or standing in the toy minefield. Pause. Feel your feet.

Minute Mindfulness Practice:

- **Wiggle your toes**
- **Feel the floor under your heels**
- **Shift your weight left and right**

Say to yourself:

I'M HERE. I'M SAFE. I'M OKAY.

Add a sensory check-in:

- 1 thing you can feel
- 1 thing you can smell
- 1 thing you can hear

BOOM. YOU'RE GROUNDED. NO CRYSTALS NEEDED.

Bonus ideas:
- **Stand still while washing dishes and feel the warm water.**
- **Place one hand on your chest and just breathe.**
- **Look out the window for one minute without multitasking.**

7

FLIP THE SCRIPT

(Tiny mindset resets when your brain's being mean.)

You're thinking "I'm failing," "I'm behind," or "I can't do this." Let's interrupt that.

Minute Mindfulness Practice: Mantra Swap Take one negative thought and gently replace it.

Here are some swaps:

- "I'm so behind"   I'm doing what I can with what I have.
- "I'm not patient enough"   I'm human. I care. That's enough.
- "I'm a mess"   I'm in the middle of something beautiful and hard.

Repeat your new phrase while doing a task — folding laundry, changing a nappy, picking Cheerios off the floor.

Other quick flips:

- **Write your new mantra on a Post-it and stick it on the fridge**
- **Say it into the mirror like a bossy friend who loves you**
- **Put your hand on your heart and whisper it like a secret**

These aren't cheesy. They're lifesavers in disguise.

8

THE TOY TIDY TRANCE

(Yes, you can zen out while picking up plastic broccoli.)

Toys everywhere? Before you rage clean, turn it into a moment.

Minute Mindfulness Practice:
- **Pick up one toy at a time**
- **Inhale as you bend down**
- **Exhale as you place it in the basket**
- **Match your breath to your movement**

Pretend you're doing toy yoga. You're calm. You're graceful. You are not stepping on a Lego. (Okay, maybe you are — breathe through it.)

9

THE MINDFUL HUG

(Turns out, cuddles are powerful medicine - for them and you.)

You're hugging your kid anyway — turn it into a full-body presence check.

Minute Mindfulness Practice:
- **Hug them for a full 10 seconds**
- **Notice their weight, their smell, the little heartbeat**
- **Breathe deeply**
- **Think one quiet thought: This is my reason.**

Let that hug sink in. That one moment of connection? It rewires your whole nervous system — science says so.

10

THE MIRROR RESET

(From "hot mess" to "hot mama" in one mindful minute.)

Catch yourself in the mirror looking frazzled? Pause.

Minute Mindfulness Practice:

- **Look yourself in the eye**
- **Smile (awkward is fine)**
- **Say one kind thing out loud:**
- **"You're doing better than you think."**
- **"You're still here. That counts."**
- **"You are doing your best."**

Mirror affirmations aren't woo — they're grounding. Especially on the days you forget what you look like without baby food on your top.

THE DISH SOAP MEDITATION

(Because if you're gonna be elbow-deep in bubbles, you may as well be present.)

You're doing dishes — again. Might as well turn it into mindfulness.

Minute Mindfulness Practice:

- **Focus on the warmth of the water**
- **Feel the slipperiness of the suds**
- **Watch the way bubbles float and pop**
- **Let your breath match your movements**

It's simple. It's repetitive. And for a moment, it's quiet. That's a mindfulness win.

12

THE BEDTIME BREATH

(When they're finally asleep and you don't know what to do with yourself.)

The house is quiet. You're wiped. Instead of doom scrolling, pause.

Minute Mindfulness Practice:
- **Sit on the edge of your bed or couch**
- **Place one hand on your heart**
- **Inhale deeply**
- **As you exhale, say: Let go.**
- **Repeat for one minute**

Let go of the chaos, the guilt, the to-do list.

You've done enough today.

YOU ARE ENOUGH.

13

THE "NOT NOW" NOD

(Because you don't need to solve everything right this second.)

When your brain starts spinning with all the things you "should" be doing, try this:

Minute Mindfulness Practice:
- **Place your hand over your chest or belly**
- **Take one breath and say (out loud or in your head):**
- **"Not now. I'll get to it. But not now."**

This helps stop the spiral. You don't need to fix it. You just need to pause.

14

THE SOCK SORT STILLNESS

(Laundry + peace = possible? Yep.)

Sorting socks = a weirdly good time to breathe and reset.

Minute Mindfulness Practice:

- **Match socks slowly**
- **Notice textures, patterns, tiny holes**
- **Breathe as you go**
- **Let yourself be present with this small, boring, beautiful task**

Bonus: oddly satisfying.

15

THE KITCHEN WINDOW MINUTE

(When you need to remember there's a world beyond dishes and school lunches.)

Stand at the window. Just stand there.

Minute Mindfulness Practice:
- **Look out. Don't think. Just observe.**
- **See the light, clouds, plants, laundry flapping.**
- **Imagine your thoughts drifting away with the breeze.**

Let the view be your meditation. Even if it's just your neighbour's bin.

16

THE "TINY CELEBRATION" TRICK

(You brushed your kid's hair without a tantrum? That's a win.)

We rush past wins. Let's change that.

Minute Mindfulness Practice:

- **Pick one small thing you did well today (anything counts)**
- **Smile. Say "Well done, Mama."**
- **Raise your coffee cup or toothbrush in celebration**

Cheesy? Maybe. Powerful? Absolutely.

17

THE "STILL HERE" SIT

(This is for the moments when everything feels like too much.)

Sometimes all you can do is exist for a second.

Minute Mindfulness Practice:
- **Sit. Close your eyes.**
- **Say, slowly:**
- **"I'm still here."**
- **"I'm still breathing."**
- **"This will pass."**

You don't need to change the moment. Just survive it with awareness.

18

THE "GRATITUDE GLANCE"

(Micro gratitude = macro shift.)

You don't need a journal. Just your eyeballs.

Minute Mindfulness Practice:

- **Look around. Name 3 things you're grateful for**
- **Out loud, or in your head**
- **They can be deep (your kids) or dumb (hot chips)**

Gratitude doesn't need a paragraph. Just a pause.

19

THE "CHANGE THE CHANNEL" TRICK

(When your thoughts are being rude.)

Your brain playing greatest hits like "You're not doing enough"? Change the station.

Minute Mindfulness Practice:

- **Say "No thank you, brain" out loud (yes, talk to it)**
- **Pick a mantra, like:**
- "Today is allowed to be easy."
- "I'm doing what I can."

Rinse, repeat. Tune out the static.

20

THE "ONE THING" SCAN

(Overwhelmed? Shrink it.)

You've got 57 tabs open in your brain. Time to pick one.

Minute Mindfulness Practice:
- **Ask: What's the one thing I need right now?**
- **Not ten things. Just one.**
- **A glass of water? A breath? A stretch?**

Name it. Do it. Breathe. The rest can wait.

21

THE "MINDFUL MESS" REFRAME

(That pile of chaos? It means life is happening.)

Instead of sighing at the mess, try this:

Minute Mindfulness Practice:
- **Pick one messy corner**
- **Look at it without judgment**
- **Say: This means we're living. It doesn't mean I'm failing.**

Then breathe in. Breathe out. Step away if needed.

22

THE "JUST SIT WITH IT" MOMENT

(You don't have to solve, fix, or figure it all out right now.)

Feeling sad, mad, or meh? Don't push it away.

Minute Mindfulness Practice:
- **Sit for one minute**
- **Say: I don't have to feel better right now. I just have to feel.**
- **Breathe with whatever's there. Let it be.**

You're not broken. You're just feeling. That's human.

23

THE "NAME IT TO TAME IT" TRICK

(Because sometimes you just need to label the chaos.)

Feel like you're spiraling? Give that feeling a name.

Minute Mindfulness Practice:

- **Pause. Ask: What am I feeling right now?**
- **Say it: "I feel overwhelmed" / "I feel tired" / "I feel pulled in every direction"**
- **Then say: It's okay to feel this way.**

Naming it reduces its power. It's not weak — it's wise.

24

THE "SLOW THE SCROLL" PAUSE

(You picked up your phone to escape. Before you scroll...)

Minute Mindfulness Practice:

- **Take one breath before unlocking your phone**
- **Ask: Am I escaping or connecting?**
- **If it's escape – fine. But make it conscious escape.**

Mindless scrolling? We've all done it. Just don't do it unconsciously. Own it. Or put the phone down. Either way = power.

25

THE "LAUNDRY BASKET SIT"

(You weren't going to sit down, so the universe gave you clean laundry to force the issue.)

Minute Mindfulness Practice:

- **Sit on the floor next to the laundry basket**
- **Let your shoulders drop**
- **Take three breaths with your hands resting on the warm clothes**
- **Feel the weight. Feel yourself land.**

Laundry = therapy, apparently.

26

THE "TINY TOUCH" TRICK

(You don't have to say anything. Just touch can say, "I'm here.")

Minute Mindfulness Practice:
- **Gently place your hand on your child's head, shoulder, or back**
- **Take one breath and feel that connection**
- **No words. Just presence.**

That one soft, quiet second? They'll remember it — and so will you.

27

THE "SNACK GRATITUDE" SHIFT

(You're eating your kid's leftover fish fingers. Let's romanticize it.)

Minute Mindfulness Practice:

- **Whatever you're eating – pause**
- **Smell it, feel it, actually taste it**
- **Say: Thank you. I have food. This is enough for now.**

Even crusty corner-toast counts. It's fuel. It's presence. It's a pause.

28

THE "LOOK UP" MOMENT

(We stare down all day. Time to look up.)

Minute Mindfulness Practice:

- **Stop what you're doing**
- **Tilt your chin up – toward the sky, the ceiling, the clouds**
- **Take one slow breath and say: There's more than this moment.**

Reminds you the world is big — and this moment isn't all there is.

29

THE "SILENT SIP & SMILE"

(Coffee. Tea. Water. Doesn't matter. Make it sacred.)

Minute Mindfulness Practice:

- **Take one sip**
- **Smile softly (even fake smiling works!)**
- **Feel that little inner lift – even if it's 1% more peace**

One smile. One sip. One shift.

30

THE "LIE DOWN ANYWAY" RESET

(You don't have time to nap. Doesn't mean you can't lie down.)

Minute Mindfulness Practice:

- Lie flat on your back for one minute
- Legs up, arms down, eyes closed if you can
- Breathe and say: I am resting. I deserve rest. One minute counts.

Because sometimes lying down (even for 60 seconds) is everything.

PART 3

Real-Life, Real-Tired Routines

Because your routine is already full – but your nervous system still needs a break.

31

MORNINGS WITH NO ZEN

(You woke up to a foot in your face. Let's recover.)

Let's be real: most mornings in mom-land don't start with journaling and lemon water. They start with a kid yelling your name, a sock crisis, and someone asking you where their homework is — even though it's clearly not taped to your forehead.

But how you start the day does matter. So let's reclaim the first 60 seconds we can grab.

One-Minute Morning Resets:

- **Before you get out of bed: Stretch, breathe in, say "I get to try again today."**
- **While brushing your teeth: Breathe through your nose, feel the floor, notice the motion.**
- **Coffee pause: Hold your mug with both hands and take three intentional sips before the chaos starts.**
- **Before waking the kids: Put your hand on your chest, say: "I'm calm. I'm kind. I'm capable." (Even if you're none of those yet.)**

It's not about changing the whole morning. It's about not letting it bulldoze you from the first step.

32

THE MIDDAY SLUMP SLAP

(No sugar crash. No crying in the car. Just one mindful minute to revive you.)

That 2-3pm feeling.
Energy = zero.
Motivation = gone.
Hope = fading.

You're either reaching for caffeine, carbs, or contemplating just lying on the floor.

Before any of that — pause.

One-Minute Midday Energy Boosters:

- The Shake-Off: Stand up, shake your arms, bounce gently on your feet, wiggle your body like you're in a toddler dance party.
- Cold Water Wake-Up: Splash your face. Feel the sensation. It's primal. It works.
- Breathe with movement: Inhale while reaching arms overhead, exhale as you fold down. Do that 5 times.
- Quick gratitude glance: Look around, name 3 things you're glad for. Even if one is just "this chair."

You don't need to "power through." You need to reset - even if it's only for 60 seconds.

33

EVENINGS AKA THE FINAL BOSS

(When bedtime feels like a hostage negotiation.)

By 7pm, your brain's mush, your patience is fried, and you're considering calling bedtime an Olympic sport. You're tired. But your body is wired. You just want to lie down and disappear into Netflix.

One-Minute Evening Wind-Downs:

- The "Day's Done" Breath: Inhale, say "let." Exhale, say "go." Repeat 5 times.
- The "Throw It Away" Trick: Write one sentence on paper that annoyed you today — then crumple it. Literally let it go.
- Gratitude rewind: Think of one good moment from the day — even if it was just a quiet coffee or no poop on the floor.
- Stretch + sigh: Lie flat. Arms out. Take a full-body stretch and release it with a deep sigh.

Even 60 seconds of this tells your body: it's over, you can rest now. And that? Changes everything.

34

MINDFULNESS IN THE MADNESS

(Yes, even in traffic. Even during the tantrum. Even mid-toy explosion.)

You don't have to escape the mess to be mindful — you just have to notice you're in it.

One-Minute Mindfulness Ideas for High-Stress Moments:
- Car chaos: Feel your hands on the wheel. Breathe slowly. Say: "I'm here. I'm safe. We're okay."
- Tantrum town: Put your hand on your chest. Don't fix — just feel. Say: "We're both having a hard time."
- Dinner meltdowns: Stir slowly. Breathe with the motion. Repeat a calming phrase in your head.
- Toy explosion zone: Sit in the middle of the mess. Don't clean. Just observe. Breathe. Remind yourself: "This is evidence of life."

Madness doesn't cancel mindfulness. In fact, that's where it matters most.

35

THE SCHOOL RUN RESET

(Because the car is full but your mind can be quiet - ish.)

You're dodging backpacks, refereeing arguments over who touched who, and navigating traffic. But even here, you can claim 60 seconds of peace.

One-Minute Practice:

- At a red light or before unbuckling your seatbelt, close your eyes (briefly), breathe deeply, and name one thing you did well this morning.
- Bonus: glance in the rearview mirror, smile at yourself. That woman? She's doing it.

36

THE SUPERMARKET MINDFULNESS WALK

(Aisle 7 = unexpected inner peace.)

Before you rage-push a trolley full of snacks you didn't mean to buy, take a beat.

One-Minute Practice:

- **As you walk, slow your pace for just one aisle.**
- **Notice colours, shapes, smells.**
- **Feel your feet hit the floor.**
- **Whisper to yourself: "I'm here. That's enough."**

Let the supermarket chaos wash over you while you glide like a peaceful grocery ninja.

37

THE "ONE MINUTE BEFORE SCREENS" RULE

(Because your phone isn't the enemy – but rushing into it might be.)

Before you scroll, reply, or check messages, stop.

One-Minute Practice:
- **Place your phone down**
- **Sit still**
- **Ask: "Do I want to react or connect?"**
- **Breathe. Then proceed – with more intention.**

Even one mindful pause can stop the doom spiral.

38

SOFT PLAY SURVIVAL MODE

(Loud, sticky, overstimulating… the kids love it. Your nervous system? Not so much.)

You're not leaving. But you can ground yourself.

One-Minute Practice:

- **Plant your feet. Feel the floor through your shoes.**
- **Watch your child for 30 seconds without distraction.**
- **Say in your head: "This is chaos. But this is love."**

Let the madness be the backdrop — your breath is the soundtrack.

39

THE KITCHEN FLOOR COLLAPSE

(You didn't plan to sit down. But now you're here. Let's make it count.)

You plop down to rest your back and end up staring at crumbs. Instead of rushing up — pause.

One-Minute Practice:
- **Sit. Let your hands rest in your lap.**
- **Let your back curve.**
- **Breathe deep into your belly.**
- **Say: "Nothing to fix. Just sitting."**

You can vacuum later. For now? You just exist. And that's more than enough.

PART 4

The Tough Days Survival Kit

For when you're done, but the day isn't.

40

WHEN YOU'RE DONE (BUT STILL HAVE TO PARENT)

(Because you can't tap out... but you can reset.)

Some days just hit different — in the worst way. You're over-touched, under-rested, emotionally fried, and there are still snacks to cut and bedtime routines to fake enthusiasm for. And yet... they still need you.

This is where one minute becomes survival.

Quick Resets to Use When You're Done:
- **Lie flat on the floor for one minute. Literally ground yourself. Let the kids climb you if they must.**
- **Stand at the window and stare outside like you're in a movie. Let the view carry you somewhere else for a few breaths.**
- **Run cold water over your hands. Look at the water. Feel it. Breathe. Come back.**
- **Put one hand on your heart, one on your belly. Whisper: "This is hard. I'm still here. That's enough."**

You're not broken. You're burnt out. And that's a very different thing.

41

WHEN YOU SNAP

(You yelled. You slammed a door. You're not a bad mom - just a human one.)

Let's normalize it: we all snap.

What matters is what comes next.

How to Recover Mid-Yell (or Right After):

- Step away — even just to the hallway. Put your hand on the wall. Feel it. Breathe.
- Say out loud: "I lost it. But I can come back now."
- Apologise, simply and gently: "I was overwhelmed. I'm sorry I yelled. I love you."
- Breathe in for 4, out for 6 — give your nervous system a soft landing.

You're allowed to have big feelings.

You're allowed to repair. That's what matters most.

Bonus: When your child sees you pause, repair, and calm — you're teaching them how to do it, too.

42

GUILT & THE INVISIBLE TO-DO LIST

(The mental load is real. Let's stop carrying it all at once.)

Mom guilt is like background music: always playing softly, always judging. Add that to the invisible to-do list — the snacks, forms, appointments, permission slips, emotional check-ins — and no wonder your brain feels like tabs are always open.

Let's lighten it — in 60 seconds.

Mindful Ways to Release the Mental Load:

- Say "I did enough today" out loud — and mean it, even if laundry's still in the machine.
- Visualise your to-do list floating away like a paper boat. Just for a minute.
- Pick one thing to leave undone — on purpose. Say: "That can wait."
- Put your hand on your chest and say: "I am not the list. I am not the mess. I am a mother doing her best."

And that is always, always, enough.

43

THE "EVERYTHING FEELS LOUD" RESET

(Even the fridge humming is too much right now.)

There are days when the world feels too loud — the toys, the chatter, the background noise in your own head.

When that overstimulation hits, do this:

One-Minute Practice:

- **Close your eyes or gently cover your ears for 30 seconds**
- **Take a deep breath in through your nose**
- **As you exhale, whisper: quiet**
- **Repeat once or twice more, slow and soft**

Even a sliver of stillness can take the edge off the sensory overload.

44

THE CRYING COMBO MOMENT

(Them. You. Maybe both. It's fine.)

Crying kid in one arm. Tears behind your eyes. You're not broken — you're human. You're full.

One-Minute Practice:
- Hold your child close (or imagine it, if they won't let you)
- Breathe together — even if it's uneven and messy
- Say, out loud or inside: We're having a hard time. But we're not alone.

Let the tears come. Then let them go. That is mindfulness.

45

WHEN YOU CAN'T BE TOUCHED ANYMORE

(AKA "please no one sit on me or lean on me for a minute.")

You love your kids. But there are moments when your skin is buzzing, and you just need space.

One-Minute Practice:
- Stand up
- Shake out your arms
- Place your hands over your own heart or belly
- Say: I need space, and that's okay.

Remind yourself: boundaries aren't selfish – they're sacred.

46

WHEN YOU JUST WANT TO RUN AWAY

(You won't. But fantasizing about a hotel room alone? Valid.)

Every mom has had the "what if I just... left for a night" thought. Don't feel guilty — just honour the feeling.

One-Minute Practice:
- Sit down. Close your eyes.
- Imagine your dream escape: the silence, the pillows, the breathing room
- Inhale slowly and say: I'm still here. But I can dream.
- Exhale and say: This moment will pass.

Even 60 seconds of mental vacation helps reset your reality.

47

WHEN YOU'RE WONDERING IF YOU'RE DOING ENOUGH

(Spoiler: You are. But let's remind your brain.)

That thought creeps in – "Am I messing them up?"

Here's your one-minute antidote:

One-Minute Practice:
- Look at a photo of your child(ren) smiling
- Breathe slowly while looking
- Say: That joy? I helped build that.
- Repeat: I am enough. This is enough.
-

You're not perfect. But they don't need perfect. They need you. Just like this.

BONUS

❧❧

BONUS: Tear-Out Pages You'll Probably Forget You Have

**But when you do find them...
you'll thank past-you.**

ONE-MINUTE MAMA TRACKER

A super simple chart where you can tick off each time you take a one-minute pause.

No pressure. No gold stars. Just a quiet "hey, I showed up for myself."

Ideas for columns:
- Did I take a breath today?
- Did I have a mindful sip?
- Did I survive school pickup without swearing (out loud)?

You can track by day, by vibe, or just doodle on it while hiding in the loo.

ONE-MINUTE MAMA TRACKER

DATE:	IDEAS	YES/NO

49

PEP TALK POST-ITS

Print these. Stick them on your fridge, mirror, or forehead. Examples:

- "You're doing your best. And that's enough."
- "This moment sucks. But it's just a moment."
- "You kept everyone alive today. Legendary."
- "They don't need perfect. They need you."
- "Yes, you're still a good mom. Even right now."

Use as many as you need. Or cover your house in them like a pep-talk wallpaper.

50

BREATHE CARDS

Quick visual guides to help you breathe like a calm, grounded, totally-has-it-together person (even if you're not that person... yet).

Card ideas:
- **Box Breathing: In 4 - Hold 4 - Out 4 - Hold 4**
- **Sigh Breaths: Big inhale, even bigger dramatic sigh**
- **5-Second Reset: Inhale "Let" / Exhale "Go"**

Stick one in your bag, your bathroom drawer, or the glovebox for emergency use.

51

"I NEED A BREAK" VOUCHERS

Let's make it official. These are for those fake bathroom trips, pretend laundry moments, or "I'm just checking something in the garage" disappearances.

Cut them out. Hand one to your partner or tape it to your forehead.

Voucher ideas:
- "This entitles Mama to 60 seconds of not being touched."
- "Redeem for one moment of silence (or an attempt at it)."
- "Good for one snack you don't have to share."
- "One guilt-free breath. No explanation required."
- "Valid for one hiding session behind a locked door."

52

ONE-MINUTE JOURNAL (OR LET'S BE HONEST, IT TOOK YOU THREE TO FIND A PEN)

This page isn't for deep insights or 10-year plans. It's just here to help you clear the fog, check in with yourself, or scream into the paper if needed.

You don't have to fill the whole thing. You don't even have to spell properly. This space is just for you.

PROMPTS:

What's one thing I need right now?

_____

_____

_____

_____

_____

_____

_____

_____

_____

_____

_____

_____

_____

_____

_____

What's taking up too much space in my head?

One small win from today:

Something I can let go of (even just for now):

A reminder I want to come back to later:

Or just scribble. Doodle. Write "I'm tired" 47 times. That works too.

53

ONE-MINUTE DOODLE PAGE

Because sometimes you don't want to journal.
 You just want to draw a sun with sunglasses, scribble a squiggle, or sketch your dream holiday (spoiler: it's quiet and no one's touching you).

This page is your:

- **Mindful moment**
- **Creative outlet**
- **Sanity-saving scribble zone**

There's no right way to use it. Just grab a pen, pencil, crayon, or eyeliner (no judgment) and go for it.

Need ideas? Try these:

- Draw how you feel today — even if it's just a scribbly cloud
- Sketch a cup of coffee and write your name on it like you're at a peaceful café
- Doodle your "Calm Corner" — real or imaginary
- Trace your hand and turn it into a flower. Or a turkey. Whatever.

Your only rule: Don't think too hard. Just doodle for a minute.

ONE WEEK OF CALM

The 7-Day Minute Mama Challenge

Because seven minutes in a week is more than you probably gave yourself last week.

You don't need an hour. You don't even need 10 minutes.

Just one calm moment a day — for one week.

Tick the box, breathe it in, and know that every minute you show up for you...

- **Day 1: Sip and Pause**

Before you pick up your phone, take one slow sip of whatever you're drinking.

Hold the mug. Feel the warmth. Breathe.
That's it. You just started the challenge.

• Day 2: The 10-Second Hug

Give your child (or partner, or even yourself!) a full 10-second hug.

No rushing. No multitasking. Just... hold.

Let the moment melt into calm.

- **Day 3: One-Minute Breathing Break**

Set a timer.

Inhale slowly. Exhale even slower.

Repeat. Nothing fancy — just you, your breath, and a bit of quiet.

- **Day 4: Guilt-Free Affirmation**

Say this out loud — yes, even if it feels weird:

"I'm doing enough."

Say it again if you need to. Say it until your brain believes you.

Day 5: Look Out the Window

Stand still. Look out the window for 60 seconds.

No phone. No cleaning. Just look.

Bonus calm points if it's raining.

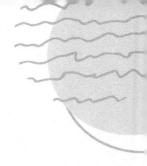

- **Day 6: Gratitude Glance**

Take one minute to name 3 things you're grateful for.

Big or small. Deep or dumb.

Gratitude rewires your brain. Even when you're wearing yesterday's T-shirt.

• Day 7: Let the Mess Be

Pick one messy thing — the floor, the laundry, your schedule — and say:

"It doesn't need to be fixed right now."

Then walk away. One minute of freedom.

HOW'D YOU DO?

Even one day counts. Even one minute counts. You're not chasing calm — you're creating it. One deep breath at a time.

WHAT HAPPENS AFTER THE WEEK?

Maybe you only did two days. Maybe you ticked all seven. Either way — you paused. You breathed. You showed up. That counts.

The hope isn't to create a perfect streak.
It's to create a tiny ritual.

A little moment you come back to — on hard days, on good ones, in between the snack demands and sock hunts.

One minute of calm, often enough... becomes a way of being.

And once it starts to feel good?

You'll find yourself doing it without even needing the reminder.

YOU'RE NOT BEHIND. YOU'RE BUILDING SOMETHING.

Keep going — one calm minute at a time.

THE MINUTE MAMA PERMISSION SLIPS

❧❧

(create permission perforated pages towards the end they can remove and stick up?)

❧❧

Because you don't need anyone's approval to take care of yourself - but just in case you forgot, here it is anyway.

✦ PERMISSION SLIPS YOU DIDN'T KNOW YOU NEEDED ✦

I give myself permission to:

- Rest, even if the house isn't clean
- Say "not right now" without guilt
- Leave the laundry for tomorrow
- Be frustrated and still be a good mom
- Order takeout and call it self-care
- Skip the playdate because I need quiet
- Feel proud of myself for surviving the day
- Say no, full stop
- Cry in the bathroom and come back stronger
- Start again at any point in the day

You don't need to earn rest. You don't have to justify your limits.

 You're allowed to just... be.

-
-
-
-
-
-
-
-
-
-
-
-
-
-
-

CLOSING

You're Doing Great, Mama

Final words from one tired, breathing, still-going mama to another.

If you've made it to the end of this book, first of all — wow. That alone deserves a trophy (or at least a hot drink you actually get to finish).

But more importantly? I hope this reminded you that mindfulness doesn't have to be another thing to get right. It's not about having a perfect routine or becoming some peaceful, whisper-voiced version of yourself.

It's about tiny pauses.
Tiny resets.

Tiny moments where you remember: I'm still here. I'm still breathing. I'm doing my best.

And that? That's enough.

You've probably already forgotten half of what's in this book — and that's okay.

Just remember this:

Every time you take a breath instead of snapping...

Every time you smile at your reflection instead of criticizing it...

Every time you pause for a minute before diving back into the madness...

That's mindfulness. That's you showing up.

So when the days are long, and your patience is shorter than your toddler's attention span, come back to your breath.

Come back to your body. Come back to you.

You're not doing it wrong. You're doing it real.

NOW GO – TAKE A MINUTE FOR YOURSELF.

— ♥ ᵥ —

OR AT LEAST GO PRETEND TO PEE ALONE.

— ♥ ᵥ —

✨ **YOU'VE EARNED IT.** ✨

Made in the USA
Coppell, TX
18 May 2025

49463021R00066